Classroom Guitar for School Music Programs:

Guitar Group I, II, III and IV

T0116895

Walking in Harmony
Level I

by

Richard Tyborowski

AuthorHouse™
1663 Liberty Drive
Bloomington, IN 47403
www.authorhouse.com
Phone: 1-800-839-8640

First published by AuthorHouse 11/24/2010

ISBN: 978-1-4520-8464-0 (sc)
ISBN: 978-1-4520-8465-7 (e)

Library of Congress Control Number 2010918317

Printed in the United States of America

This book is printed on acid-free paper.

Classroom Guitar for School Music Programs

Classroom Guitar for
School
Music Programs:
About the Author

Richard Tyborowski, originally from Poland, now lives and works in Winnipeg. He has performed on classical guitar on numerous occasions in both Canada and Europe. In recognition of his talent He has received numerous grants and scholarships. He teaches classical guitar at the Marcel A. Desautels Faculty of Music at the University of Manitoba.

His first CD, *Romantico*, was released by GFI in 1996, shortly after he moved to Winnipeg. His second CD*, Hommenage a Chopin* released by GFI in 1999, included a world premier recording of Polish composer Stanislaw Mronski's suite in homage to Chopin. *Pearls and Yarn*, released by Summit Records in 2010, featured the chamber music of the Serbian clarinetist and composer Boki Milosovic. Richard's fourth CD *Sefarad*, released by Marquis Records in 2008, contains compositions by Winnipeg's composer Sid Rabinovitch. Richard's latest effort is *Memories* by the Synergy Duo of him and the Balkan classical/jazz bassist Nenad Zdjelar. The CD contains mostly original compositions based on Balkan and Slavic music.

TABLE OF CONTENTS

Down by the Station p.40	*Down by the Station p.43*	*Down by the Station p.46*	*Down by the Station p.49*
New Notes to Learn p.41	*New Notes to Learn p.44*	*New Notes to Learn p.47*	*New Notes to Learn p.50*
Next Note p.41	*Next Note p.44*	*Next Note p.47*	*Next Note p.50*
Country Walk p.41	*Country Walk p.44*	*Country Walk p.47*	*Country Walk p.50*
Spot the Dots p.41	*Spot the Dots p.44*	*Spot the Dots p.47*	*Spot the Dots p.50*

GUITAR I	GUITAR II	GUITAR III	GUITAR IV
Eighth Note Encounter p.59	*Eighth Note Encounter p.62*	*Eighth Note Encounter p.65*	*Eighth Note Encounter p.68*
New Notes to Learn p.59	*New Notes to Learn p.62*	*New Notes to Learn p.65*	*New Notes to Learn p.68*
Skip to My Lou p.59	*Skip to My Lou p.62*	*Skip to My Lou p.65*	*Skip to My Lou p.68*
Hush Little Baby p.59	*Hush Little Baby p.62*	*Hush Little Baby p.65*	*Hush Little Baby p.68*
William Tell p.60	*William Tell p.63*	*William Tell p.66*	*William Tell p.69*
New Notes to Learn p.60	*New Notes to Learn p.63*	*New Notes to Learn p.66*	*New Notes to Learn p.69*
In the key of G Major p.60	*In the key of G Major p.63*	*In the key of G Major p.66*	*In the key of G Major p.69*
Good King Wenceslas p.61	*Good King Wenceslas p.64*	*Good King Wenceslas p.67*	*Good King Wenceslas p,70*
Alouette p.61	*Alouette p.64*	*Alouette p.67*	*Alouette p,70*
In the key of D Major p.61	*In the key of D Major p.64*	*In the key of D Major p.67*	*In the key of D Major p.70*
One Step at a Time p.61	*One Step at a Time p.64*	*One Step at a Time p.67*	*One Step at a Time p.70*

GUITAR I	GUITAR II	GUITAR III	GUITAR IV
When the Saints Go Marching In Exercise I p.73	*When the Saints Go Marching In Exercise I p.80*	*When the Saints Go Marching In Exercise I p.87*	*When the Saints Go Marching In Exercise I p.93*
When the Saints Go Marching in Exercise II p.73	*When the Saints Go Marching in Exercise II p.80*	*When the Saints Go Marching in Exercise II p.87*	*When the Saints Go Marching in Exercise II p.93*
When the Saints Go Marching In p.73	*When the Saints Go Marching In p.80*	*When the Saints Go Marching In p.87*	*When the Saints Go Marching In p.93*
Minor Rock p.74	*Minor Rock p.81*	*Minor Rock p.88*	*Minor Rock p.94*
Kum Ba Yah Exercise I Rhythm p.74	*Kum Ba Yah Exercise I Rhythm p.81*	*Kum Ba Yah Exercise I Rhythm p.88*	*Kum Ba Yah Exercise I Rhythm p.94*
Kum Ba Yah p.75	*Kum Ba Yah p.82*	*Kum Ba Yah p.88*	*Kum Ba Yah p.95*
Amigos Exercise I p.75	*Amigos Exercise I p.82*	*Amigos Exercise I p.89*	*Amigos Exercise I p.95*
Amigos Exercise II p.75	*Amigos Exercise II p.82*	*Amigos Exercise II p.89*	*Amigos Exercise II p.95*
Amigos p.76	*Amigos p.83*	*Amigos p.89*	*Amigos p.96*
Aria p.77	*Aria p.84*	*Aria p.90*	*Aria p.97*
Scarborough Fair p.77	*Scarborough Fair p.84*	*Scarborough Fair p.90*	*Scarborough Fair p.97*
Variations on a Theme by Mozart p.78	*Variations on a Theme by Mozart p.85*	*Variations on a Theme by Mozart p.91*	*Variations on a Theme by Mozart p. 98*
Spring Song p.79	*Spring Song p.86*	*Spring Song p.92*	*Spring Song p.99*
Dance p.79	*Dance p.86*	*Dance p.92*	*Dance p.99*

INTRODUCTION

For over twenty years of my professional life, I have taught guitar at all levels from introductory to postgraduate. When I was first asked to teach in the Grades 5-8 School Guitar Program, I was both excited at the prospect and apprehensive about the challenges ahead. I had never taught in such environment before, and I wondered how my knowledge of the guitar world would resonate with large groups of children. The first year turned out to be a string of mini-disasters, at least from my point of view. This situation was not caused by a lack of interest or enthusiasm on the part of the students. They did their best trying to play the same solo piece together, but the result was lamentable. Some played faster, and others slower. Those who could not keep up started to complain, and a few gave up trying. While the more advanced students started playing more complicated pieces, others got frustrated and started dropping the course. At best, the class was able to perform a simple piece with my accompaniment, but it was always an uphill struggle and little fun.

Obviously, I needed to change something and, upon reflection, decided to change my Guitar Class to a Guitar Orchestra. In a guitar ensemble, it is less important how difficult the notes are and much more important how different notes are performed together. Once I adopted and implemented this principle, my Guitar Orchestra started sounding much better from the very first note. Instead of playing the same notes together, students started playing in four voice harmony. They began by each group learning a different note, and then playing together to sound a chord. This approach created more interest and, of course, more attention among students. That initial success was also the starting point of this book.

In addition to a core orchestra program, this book also offers a number of solo pieces. These pieces allow a degree of flexibility in dealing with students performing at different levels of ability. The music I have selected comes from a wide range of musical cultures. Some pieces may work for the entire class, but their most important role is to help develop students' individual skills, especially in the area of hand and body position. Since this textbook is only a starting point, a visit to a local music store is a must, supplementing with a few volumes of current popular styles will allow students to apply their new guitar skills to the music of their choice. Even with group playing, it is important to devote some time to individual players as there is no substitute for one to one instruction.

The main focus of this book, however, is on playing together. The ensemble experience will develop students' ability to perform individual parts while, at the same time, listening to others. In the long run, the ability to work in a group will enhance young people's chances to achieve their goals in life, whether they lie within the sphere of music or outside. After all, a perfect office is like a symphony orchestra in which everyone is playing (or doing) something different, but together they accomplish a larger, more challenging and more satisfying task.

This book presents a comprehensive method that includes all aspects of music, from learning music theory, to performing different pieces, to improvising, and to composing the first piece.

All units are designed to support and inspire the growth of a child as a music maker. The teacher does not need to follow the order of this book but can choose units according to her or his needs. I have divided the book into "units" rather than "lessons" because I am aware that teaching some of them may take longer than others, depending on the size and composition of the class. Only the teacher of the classroom level can determine the number of classes needed to accomplish a given set of learning tasks.

With certain units, I recommend the teacher return to specific units as many times as she or he thinks necessary. For example, Unit 6: Creative Expression, works especially well for independent assignments and can be used for that purpose repeatedly. Some other units, such as Elements of Music, are best explained in the classroom during the lesson. However, what is most important is to let students play together. I hope this book will help open a child's creative mind with a rich, meaningful, and first-hand experience of music making. Skills acquired in this program will serve them and their communities for life.

Acknowledgement
Dr. Francine Morin, Dr. Zbigniew Izydorczyk

On Using Classroom Guitar for School Music Programs

Classroom Guitar for School Music Programs is a comprehensive classroom guitar method for group study. It is designed to be used with students who had no previous experience in guitar ensembles. In most cases, the average student will successfully complete Book 1 within two or three years.

Goals and Specific Outcomes

Setting appropriate and achievable goals for a specific grade improves the effectiveness of teaching and learning, and motivates students to practice, which is essential for success. However, it is extremely important that the goals be sound and clearly articulated, for both the teacher and the students. When planning those goals, I considered such questions as: What is the value of teaching instruments at school? To what degree should learners participate in the shaping of the curriculum? Would it be enough to teach students simple chords and some pieces of popular music? Finally, what specific outcomes should we expect after implementing those goals? When planning the goals I also took into account the knowledge students have from previous grades. Here are the most important goals indispensable for further development of the young musician. Ultimately, it will be up to the teacher to pursue all of these goals.

Goals:

1. To develop the ability to play in a guitar ensemble.
2. To develop the ability to play solo.
3. To develop the ability to improvise.
4. To develop the ability and knowledge to compose melodies.
5. To develop the ability to perform in different guitar styles.
6. To establish and improve knowledge about elements of music.
7. To develop an understanding of the basic history of the guitar.

Students will be able to:

1. Play a tune with increasing control and accuracy, and with a sense of phrasing and expression.
2. Play a variety of parts (guitar 1, 2, 3, or 4) while maintaining an individual part in a guitar ensemble.
3. Demonstrate an understanding of balance and blend in a guitar ensemble.
4. Tune the guitar using intervals or an electronic tuner.
5. Read and write some melodic and rhythmic patterns.
6. Play notes in the first and fifth positions.
7. Play a variety of scales (C, G, D and A major) and E minor - Pentatonic
8. Perform and demonstrate an understanding of more complex rhythmic concepts (such as the dotted quarter-eighth note rhythm, playing in 2/4 and 3/4 time, maintaining an individual part with a different melody and rhythm, sixteenth and eighth note combinations, and triplets).
9. Demonstrate an understanding of melodic design (root note and step-wise motion)
10. Improvise short melodies based on the pentatonic scale composing.
11. Identify the difference between major and minor chords.
12. Identify and use chord changes in two/three chord songs.
13. Search for and discover ideas for composition through experimentation and improvisation.
14. Make interpretive decisions (tempo, dynamics, articulation and tone color)
15. Share their own music with others through performance, composition portfolios, or sound/video recording of their work.
16. Perform, listen to, describe and compare music representative of different times and places.
17. Demonstrate an understanding of dynamics (crescendo and decrescendo, pp, p, mp, mf, f, and ff) well as expressive accent (>).
18. Play a variety of chords.

The Instrument: CLASSICAL GUITAR

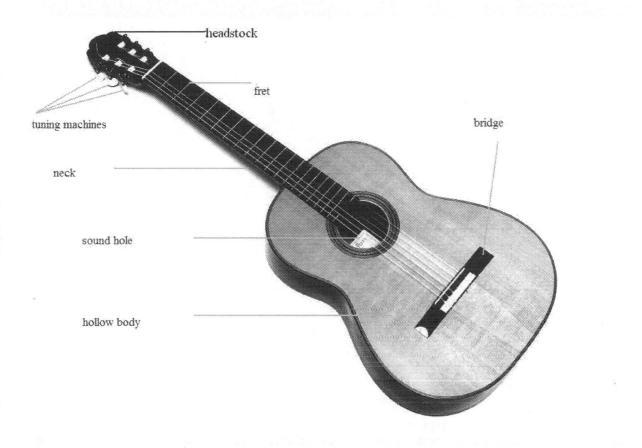

headstock

fret

tuning machines

bridge

neck

sound hole

hollow body

The classical, or Spanish, guitar is the most widely used type of guitar. It consists of a hollow body with a sound hole, a neck with frets, and a headstock with tuning machines.

String	Note
1st string (thinnest)	E
2nd string	B
3rd string	G
4th string	D
5th string	A
6th string (thickest)	E

9

HOW TO TUNE GUITAR

Tuning by Interval

To begin with, the open 5th string should be tuned to the note A Tune A string to a tuning fork, or piano, then place your finger at the fifth fret of the sixth string and press down. The pitch should be the same like an open string A. Adjust tuning of the sixth string accordingly. Do the same with all others with the exception of the third string, where you need to press fourth fret instead. When the guitar is in tune, the open 2nd string (B) can be tuned an octave below the B played on the 7th fret of the 1st string.

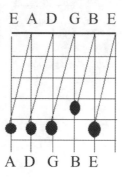

Tuning with an electronic tuner

There are many electronic tuners on the market today. An electronic tuner monitors the frequency of each of the six strings.

Tune slowly and carefully.

1st	E	Open
2nd	B	Open
3rd	G	Open
4th	D	Open
5th	A	Open
6th	E	Open

Unit 1: Guitar Technique

Before you start, you must remember some fundamentals:

- There is nothing unnatural about playing the guitar. What we are trying to do is to develop the ability you **already possess**. It is true that some people, when they start plying the guitar on their own (without the assistance of a qualified teacher), make so many mistakes that it may take years to correct their bad habits. This usually happens when the beginning players do not pay enough attention to their natural motions.
- Your left and right hands work in the same way. Imagine that you are squeezing a ball, and look how your fingers work because this is exactly the way you are going to play the guitar. Practice it many times without the guitar (and without the ball); just imagine that you are playing with it. Then, as you start playing the guitar, always remember what you have learned from that exercise, and compare how your fingers work with and without the guitar.
- Always listen to the tone you produce on the guitar. Good tone is the sign that you are on the right path and that you are acquiring proper technique.
- Tension is your greatest enemy, and you need to do everything to get rid of it. Feel the rhythm of your music, stay relaxed and natural.
- Remember that every sound is produced in three steps: **preparation – stroke – relaxation**, no matter how fast you are playing.
- When playing scales, alternate your fingers, as you do with your legs when walking. Avoid always playing with the same finger.

Sitting Position

Begin by sitting up straight on the edge of a chair. Your back should be straight, aligning the back muscles with the spine. Your shoulders should be relaxed and level. The objective here is good basic posture, avoiding any slouching, leaning against the back of the chair, hunching or twisting your shoulders.

Adjust the footstool to about seven inches in height and place it on the floor, aligning it with the left side legs of the chair, just beneath your left leg. Place your left foot on the footstool and adjust it forwards or backwards so that your lower leg is perpendicular to the floor. Also, adjust the height of the footstool so that the upper leg is pointing slightly upwards. After you have properly positioned your footstool and placed your left foot upon it, check again to make sure that you feel no tension or misalignment in your back or shoulders.

Next, hold the guitar in a comfortable and secure playing position, making sure that each hand has good access to the strings and to the full range of the fingerboard.

The Rested Stroke

The rested stroke is a good way to learn the proper way of producing a tone. The finger strokes the high E string, for instance, and comes to rest on string B (the second string). In the rested stroke, the nail curves around the string as it passes over it. Always be careful to keep the first knuckle joint of the finger supple (not stiff).

The Free Stroke

The free stroke is used most frequently. The free stroke should be practiced from the slowest tempo to the most rapid. Always be careful to create a round, full tone at all speeds. The right hand fingers bend slightly during the free stroke (they do not bend in the rested stroke). Make sure you move the fingers of both hands as little as possible while practicing. The more your fingers move away from the strings as you play, the longer it takes them to get back to the string when it is time to play that string again. Minimal movement of both hands is what allows rapid playing.

Unit 2: Elements of Music 1

Staff		A staff consists of five parallel, equidistant lines with spaces in between.
The whole note **The whole rest**	The whole note The whole rest	With 4/4 time signature, the whole note is four counts of sound. The whole rest is four counts of silence.
Bar lines **Measure**	< Measure >	A vertical line is placed in a staff to mark off measures. A measure is the space between two bar lines.
Notes	F A C E E G B D F F E G	The lines designate the following notes, starting from the bottom: E, G, B, D, F. This is easily remembered by using the mnemonic "Every Good Boy Does Fine" The spaces between the lines represent the notes F, A, C, E, starting from the bottom.
Treble clef		The treble clef is also called the "G" clef because the loop at the bottom wraps around the line on a staff for the G note above middle C.
Ledger lines		Ledger lines are the lines added above or below the staff.

Let's talk about legers lines,

Do you remember the sentence, "Every Good Boy Does Fine", or "Every Good Boy Deserves Fudge" and the word "FACE". Well, we can use them with ledger lines as well, but this time E,G,B,D,F will be on spaces below the staff

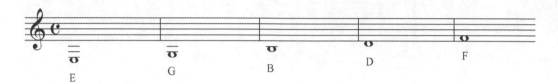

as well as above the staff.

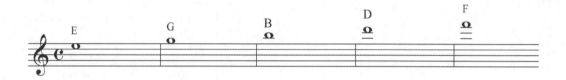

F,A,C,E will indicate lines below the staff

as well as above.

Performance Skills 1: Exercises Guitar I

LET'S START
Open your case right side up, pick up your guitar, sit on the chair, adjust your footstool and open the first exercise.

Guitar Group I
Let's begin with three notes on the first string.

The E note is played on the open **first** string. You do not use any left hand fingers to play this note; you simply pick the first string. For the F note, place your 1st finger at the first fret (that is, close to the first fret, but not on the fret itself) and press down. The G note is played using your 3rd finger at the third fret (again, place your 3rd finger close to the fret but not directly on it). Try to use the tips of your fingers and make sure the notes ring clean after you pick them (no buzzing).

THE FIRST NOTE -E

This is a "whole" note. It has an open note head and no stem. In 4/4 time, a whole note gets held for four beats.

THE SECOND NOTE -F

15

THE THIRD NOTE- G

WHOLE LOTTA COUNTING

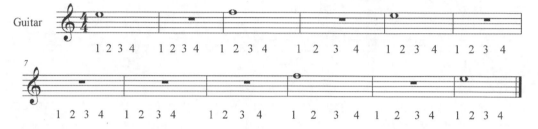

STEP BY STEP

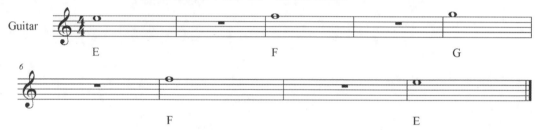

WHAY CAN'T YOU JUST JUMP

ROCK GUITAR

DAWN AND DAWN

UP AND DAWN

Performance Skills 1: Exercises Guitar II

LET'S START
Open your case right side up, pick up your guitar, sit on the chair, adjust your footstool and open the first exercise.

Guitar Group 2
Let's begin with three notes on the second string.

The B note is played on the open **second** string. You do not use any left hand fingers to play this note; you simply pick the second string. For the C note, place your 1st finger at the first fret (that is, close to the first fret, but not on the fret itself) and press down. The D note is played using your 3rd finger at the third fret (that is, place your 3rd finger close to the fret but not directly on it). Try to use the tips of your fingers and make sure the notes ring clean after you pick them (no buzzing).

THE FIRST NOTE B

This is a "whole" note. It has an open note head and no stem. In 4/4 time, a whole note gets held for four beats.

THE SECOND NOTE C

For the C note, place your 1st finger at the first fret.

THE THIRD NOTE D

The D note is played using your 3rd finger at the third fret.

WHOLE LOTTA COUNTING

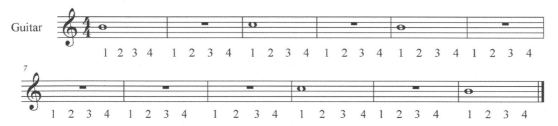

STEP BY STEP

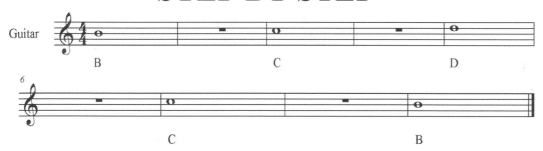

WHY CAN'T YOU JUST JUMP

ROCK GUITAR

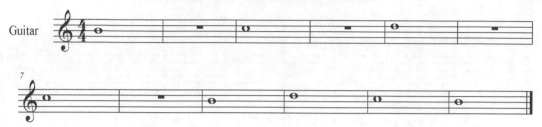

DAWN AND DAWN

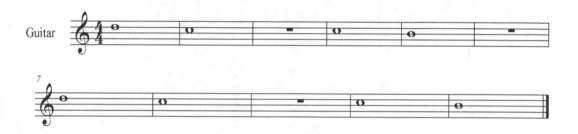

UP AND DAWN

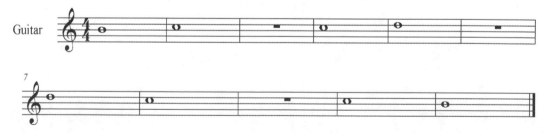

Performance Skills 1: Exercises Guitar III

LET'S START

Open your case right side up, pick up your guitar, sit on the chair, adjust your footstool and open the first exercise.

Guitar Group 3

Three notes on the third string.

The G note is an open third string note. You don't use any fingers to play this note, you just pick the 3rd string. For the A note, place your 2nd finger at the 2nd fret (place your finger close to the 2nd fret, but not on it, and press down.) The B note is played on open second string.

THE FIRST NOTE -G

THE SECOND NOTE - A

21

THE THIRD NOTE - B

WHOLE LOTTA COUNTING

STEP BY STEP

WHY CAN'T YOU JUST JUMP

ROCK GUITAR

DAWN AND DAWN

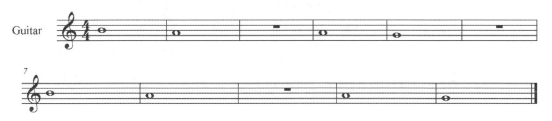

UP AND DAWN

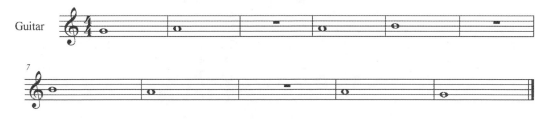

Performance Skills 1: Exercises Guitar IV

LET'S START

Open your case right side up, pick up your guitar, sit on the chair, adjust your footstool and open the first exercise.

Let's begin with three notes on the sixth string.

The E note is played on the open **sixth** string. You do not use any left hand fingers to play this note; you simply pick the first string. For the F note, place your 1st finger at the 1st fret (that is close to the 1st fret, but not on it), and press down. The G note is played using your 3rd finger at the 3rd fret. Again, place your 3rd finger close to the fret but not on it. Try to use the tips of your fingers and make sure the notes ring clean after you pick them (no buzzing).

THE FIRST NOTE -E

This is a "whole" note. It has an open note head and no stem. In 4/4 time, a whole note gets held for four beats.

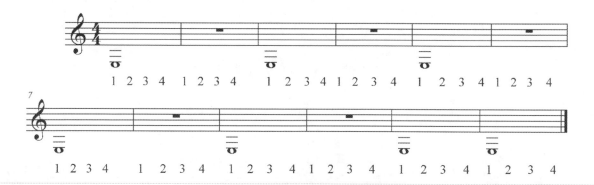

THE SECOND NOTE -F

24

THE THIRD NOTE- G

WHOLE LOTTA COUNTING

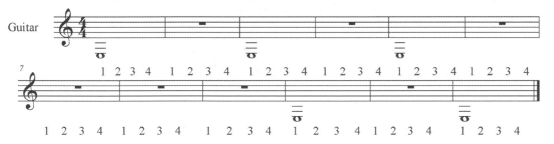

STEP BY STEP

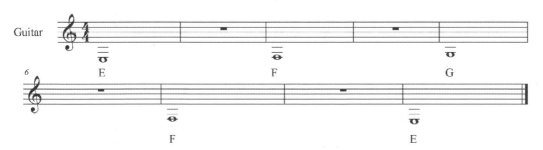

WHAY CAN'T YOU JUST JUMP

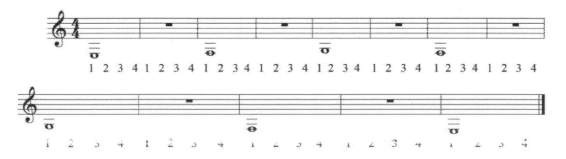

25

ROCK GUITAR

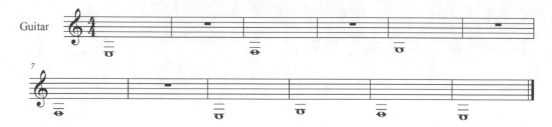

DAWN AND DAWN

UP AND DAWN

Unit 3: Music in Context - History of the Guitar

Guitar Exhibit

- Classical / Spanish guitar

The classical, or Spanish, guitar is the most widely used kind of guitar. It consists of a hollow body with sound hole, and a neck with tuning machines/headstock. Typically, the classical guitar uses nylon strings, which make them easy to use for both plucking and strumming. Classical guitars are used when playing in classical, Latin, Flamenco (hence the name Spanish guitar), and other popular styles of music.

- Acoustic or steel string guitar

At first sight, the acoustic guitar is very similar to the classical guitar. Sometimes both kinds of guitar are referred to as acoustic guitar because they both produce sound without any amplifiers. In contrast to the classical guitar, the acoustic guitar uses steel strings. Its neck is smaller, and it is often equipped with an electric sound system. Typically, a plectrum is used to play an acoustic guitar. This kind of guitar is typically used in pop music as an accompanying instrument.

- Electric steel string guitar

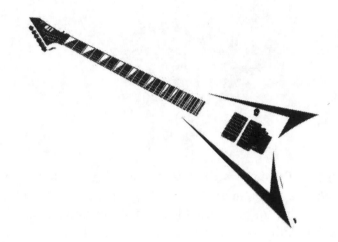

The electric guitar uses electricity to produce its sound through an amplifier. In contrast to acoustic guitars, the electric guitar does not have a sound hole; instead, it consists of a board-like body. The electric guitar uses steel strings that, when played, produce vibrations that are received by pick-ups. The electric guitar is a typical rock instrument because it can create massive sounds when amplified.

These three types of guitars not only look different, but they also represent different playing styles. The classical guitar is always played with the fingers, while the other two are played with picks and only occasionally the fingers.

Classical Guitar Periods

- RENAISSANCE PERIOD   (1450 - 1600)
  The Renaissance was a time of rebirth and massive cultural upheaval. Music was influenced by the general receptivity to new ideas. During this time, guitar was used for chording in song accompaniment or in dance music. The most popular forms of dance music in that era were pavanes, galliards, and the almandes. The only purely instrumental guitar form at that time was the fantasy. At the beginning of the Renaissance, some composers did not reveal their real names; instead, they signed themselves as Anonymous. But there were also very important names we need to remember, such as John Dowland (1563-1626), Luis Milan (1500- 1561) (Spain) Alonso de Mudarra (1508-1580) (Spain), Adrien le Roy (15201598) (France), Melchior Neusidler (1531-1590) (Germany), William Byrd (1543-1623) (UK), Jakub Polak (1545?-1605) (Poland), and many others.

- BAROQUE PERIOD
  The term Baroque describes the style of European music between 1600 and 1750. The music of this time period was characterized by rich counterpoint and a highly decorated melodic line. The most important characteristics of this era are the use of the basso continuo, the belief in the doctrine of the affections, as well as the emphasis on contrast of volume, texture, and pace in the music. In keeping with the elaborate styles of the Baroque era, music for the guitar incorporated many of those characteristics. The names we need to remember include: Johann Sebastian Bach (1685-1750) (Germany), Robert de Visée (c.1650- 1725) (Portugal), Antonio Vivaldi (1680-1743) (Italy), Luigi Boccherini (1743-1805) (Italy), Scarlatti, Domenico (1685-1757) (Italy), Silvius Leopold Weiss (1686-1750) (Germany), Johann Anton Logy(1650-1721) (Bohemia), Francesco Corbetta (1615-1681) (Italy), Gaspar Sanz (1640-1710) (Spain).

- CLASICAL PERIOD
  The Classical period in music extended from 1750 to 1820 and it was defined by structure. Even before the death of JS Bach, there was a movement towards replacing majestic splendor by graceful delicacy. If Baroque music is notable for its textural intricacy, the Classical music is characterized by a near-obsession with its structural clarity. The search for intellectual freedom was to be the main principle of this new age of enlightenment. During this era, the six-string guitar becomes most common. The structure of the guitar had changed. The waist of the guitar was made deeper and the number of frets increased to as many as nineteen. Classical era was the Golden Era for the guitar, with virtuoso guitarists such as Fernando Sor, (1778-1839) (Spain), Ferdinando Carulli, (1770-1841) (Italy), Mauro Giuliani, (1781-1829)) (Italy), Wenzeslaus Matiegka (1773-1830) (Czech), Niccolo Paganini (1782-1840) (Italy), Dionisio Aguado (1784-1849) (Spain).

- ROMANTIC PERIOD
  The era of Romantic music is defined as the period of European classical music that runs from 1815 to 1910. Romantic music is related to romanticism in literature, visual arts, and philosophy. Unfortunately, Romantic period marked a decline in the prominence of the guitar in Europe mostly because of the increasing interest in the piano, but at the same time guitar enjoyed enormous popularity in South America. Guitar needed to wait to the end of this period to gather strength. Two independently working artist of that period are the late romantic guitarist and composer **Francisco Tarrega**(1852-1909) from Spain and the Paraguayan neo-romantic guitarist-composer **Augustin Barrios** Mangoré (1885-1944).

- FURTHER DEVELOPMENTS
  At the beginning of 20-th century, we observe a significant renaissance of guitar in Europe, first in classical and then in popular music. Andres Segovia, one of the great performers of the guitar was largely responsible for this new beginning. Segovia performed, transcribed, taught and discovered a tremendous amount of music. He also encouraged many composers to write for the guitar. He was the first person to perform in a concert hall. Before Segovia, people believed this could not be done. Today there are many concerts of guitar music. There are also many societies and magazines devoted to the guitar. A few names we need to remember includes; Andres Segovia, John Williams, Julian Bream, David Russell, Assad Brothers, and from Canada Norbert Kraft and Liona Boyd.

Unit 4: Elements of Music 2

Types of Notes

Since most of these elements were covered in previous grades, this is a review. The teacher can decide what needs to be reviewed or introduced.

An important part of learning about music is becoming familiar with the types and values of notes. This unit will remind you of what notes look like and how they sound.

The whole note	
The half note looks like a hat	
The quarter note	
The eighth note Eighth notes can also be put in groups of 4, 3, or 2 connected by a horizontal line.	
The sixteenth note Sixteenth notes can also be grouped in 2, 3 or 4 but are then joined by a double line.	

Types of Rests For each type of note you have learned, there is a corresponding rest.

The whole rest	
The half rest	looks like a hat
The quarter rest	
The eighth rest	
The sixteenth rest	

32

A Review of Basic Counting

You may wonder how musicians interpret musical symbols when they play. In part, they learn to read and count rhythms. You already learned about counting in previous grades, however the way you learned to count may be different then what you will see below. This is the most common way of counting among musicians in the West today.

In 4/4 (common rhythm)

1 whole note A *whole note* represents 4 quarter notes: four fourths, which lasts as long as a measure.

   1   2   3   4

2 half notes A *half note* represents 2 quarter notes: two fourths, half of a measure.

   1   2   3   4

4 quarter notes A *quarter note* is one of the most common note values; it represents 1/4 of a measure, or one beat.

8 eights notes An *eighth note* is the second most common note value; it represents half of a quarter note. Count "one – and – two – and – three – and – four – and" aloud; these are eighth notes, both the numbers and the "ands."

1 and 2 and 3 and 4   and

16 sixteen notes A *sixteenth note* is half of an eighth note. Count "one - e - and - a - two - e - and - a - three - e - and - a - four - e - and - a" aloud; these are sixteenth notes, each number, 'e', 'and', and 'a' (pronounced 'ah').

1 e & a   2 e & a   3 e & a   4 e & a

When we combine the 2 quarter notes and a half note, as in the example below, the half note gets the first 2 beats, and each quarter gets its own beat. This makes sense: since the 4/4 time signature means there are 4 quarter notes per measure, 2 quarter notes + 1 half note (which really equals 2 quarters) = 4 quarter notes.

1   2   3   4

How to play dotted notes

Once students have mastered the simple straight beats you should challenge them to understand and execute dotted notes accurately. Modern music utilizes this type of rhythm much more than traditional music. For example, play **COUNTRY WALK** or **CARDIFF BY THE SEA**, while you tape a toe on each beat. You'll see that the melody sticks to the counted beats 1-2-3-4 quite closely. By adding dots you move the accent from the beat to the "off beats". Off beats is the name we use to describe the moment in time between each beat. Now play after 3 on the "and".

1 + 2 + 3 + 4 +   1 + 2 + 3 + 4 +   1 + 2 + 3 + 4 +   1 + 2 + 3 + 4 +

Rhythm Game

Same of you will clap; use whole body movement to maintain a steady beat (quarter notes) while others perform different note values or rhythms accurately while reading.

Exercise I

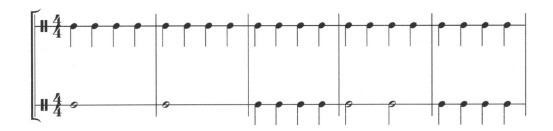

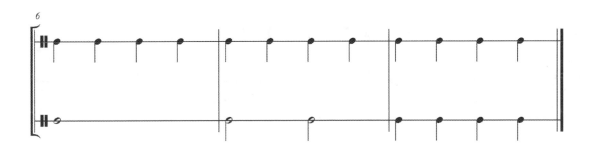

Exercise II

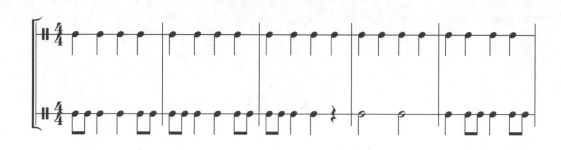

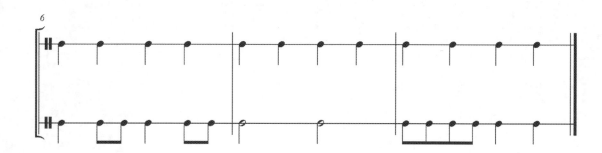

Exercise III

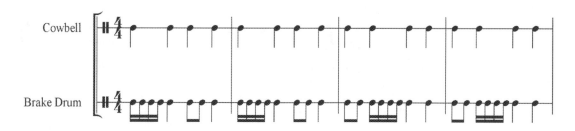

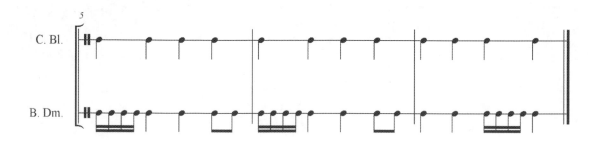

Exercise IV

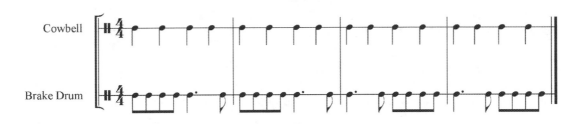

Exercise V

Exercise VI

Exercise VII

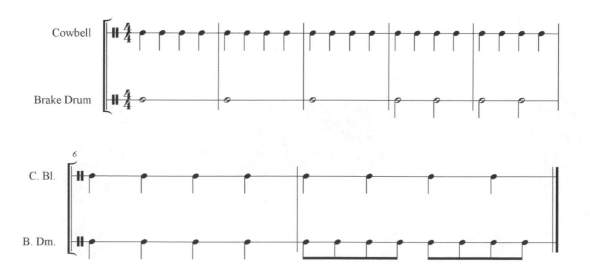

Performance Skills 2: Exercises Guitar I

The first guitar should now start playing in the fifth (written as V) position.
The fifth position means basically that the first finger is on the fifth fret.
Students will play these notes in the fifth position like this:

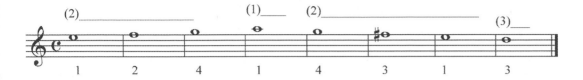

Place your first finger at the fifth fret of the second string. For the F note, place your
2nd finger at the 6th fret of the same string. The G note is played using your
4th finger at the 8th fret. For the A note, place your first finger on the fifth fret of the first string. The
F# note is played using 3rd finger at the 7th fret of the second string.

HALF THE PRICE

Half note and half rest

ONE FOR QUARTER

Quarter note - one count of sound

NEW NOTE TO LEARN A

For the A note, place your 1st finger at the 5th fret (place your finger close to the 5th fret, but not on it,
and press down.

CARDIFF BY THE SEA

Welsh folk Song

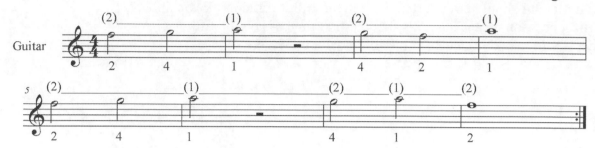

HOT CROSS BUNS

English folk Song

AU CLAIRE DE LA LUNE

French folk Song

DOWN BY THE STATION

NEW NOTES TO LEARN

D
The D note is played using your 3rd finger 2nd string.

F#
For the F sharp note, place your 2nd finger at the 3rd fret the 2nd fret on the 1st string.

NEXT NOTE

COUNTRY WALK

English Folk Song

SPOT THE DOTS

Performance Skills 2: Exercises Guitar II

HALF THE PRICE
Half note and half rest

Half note is two counts of sound and half rest is two counts of silence.

ONE FOR QUARTER
Quarter note - one count of sound

NEW NOTE TO LEARN E

The E note is an open first string note. You don't use any fingers to play this note; you just pick the 1st string.

CARDIFF BY THE SEA

Welsh folk Song

HOT CROSS BUNS

English folk Song

AU CLAIRE DE LA LUNE

French folk Song

DOWN BY THE STATION

Traditional

43

NOTES TO LEARN

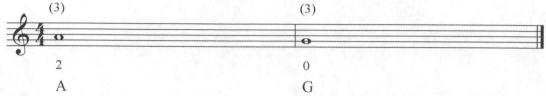

For the A note, place your 2nd finger at the second fret on the **third** string and press down. The G note is played on the open **third** string. You do not use any left hand fingers to play this note; you simply pick the third string.

NEXT NOTE

COUNTRY WALK

English Folk Song

SPOT THE DOTS

Performance Skills 2: Exercises Guitar III
HALF THE PRICE

Half note is two counts of sound and half rest is two counts of silence.

ONE FOR QUARTER

Quarter note - one count of sound

NEW NOTE TO LEARN C

For the C note, place your 1st finger at the 1st fret (place your finger close to the 1st fret, but not on it, and press down.) the 2nd string.

CARDIFF BY THE SEA

Welsh folk Song

HOT CROSS BUNS

English folk Song

AU CLAIRE DE LA LUNE

French folk Song

DOWN BY THE STATION

Traditional

NEW NOTES TO LEARN F#, E

NEXT NOTE

COUNTRY WALK

English Folk Song

SPOT THE DOTS

Performance Skills 2: Exercises Guitar IV

HALF THE PRICE

Half note is two counts of sound and half rest is two counts of silence.

ONE FOR QUARTER

Quarter note - one count of sound

NEW NOTE TO LEARN A

The A note is an open fifth string note. You don't use any fingers to play this note; just pick the 5th string.

CARDIFF BY THE SEA

Welsh folk Song

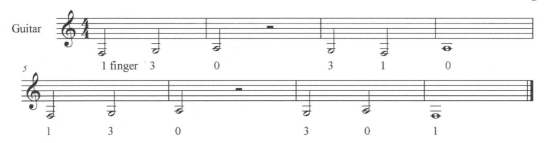

HOT CROSS BUNS

English folk Song

AU CLAIRE DE LA LUNE

French folk Song

DOWN BY THE STATION

Traditional

NEW NOTES TO LEARN

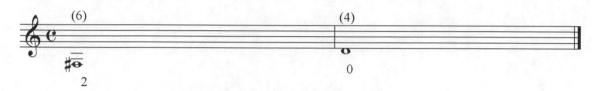

NEXT NOTE

COUNTRY WALK

English Folk Song

SPOT THE DOTS

50

Unit 5: Creative Expressions

When practicing chords, do not practice all chords at once; rather, play one or two at a time and try combining them with scales (for example, C and G chords with C scale).

Chords and Scales

Exercise 1

Let's start with the key of C major. Basic chords for this key are:

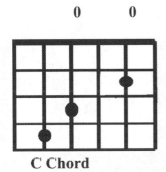

C Chord

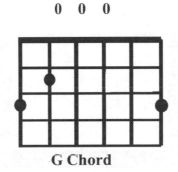

G Chord

The C major scale looks like this:

What is a scale? We can say that scales are building blocks of melodies.

What is a melody? A melody is a tune of series of notes succession occurring in time, that sounds pleasant. It is the linear aspect of music.

When first learning a scale, it is important to start and stop on the **_root note_** (tonic), which is the note that the scale is based upon. Remember that we built our scale starting on C. Play the scale and listen to how all the notes in the scale resolve to the root.

Now let's try the following experiment: Play C (root note) several times and listen carefully to how it sounds. Then play the note above (D) and the note below (B) the root. Did you notice that it sounded tense? Now again play the full scale of C Major and pay attention to how all the notes you play naturally lead to the C.

Play this once more, but this time play from the higher C to the lower one. Don't the notes again lead to the C? Now play again, but this time stop on B for a moment and notice how unfinished the scale sounds, and then notice how complete the scale sounds when you finally play the C. This is called **_resolution_**. Playing up and down the scale is a good practice, but it is not really making music.

So let's make some music! This time do not just play up and down the scale. Instead, try jumping around to different spots in the scale and see if you can come up with anything that sounds interesting.

Now play chord C Major and then play any notes you wish in the scale. Did you notice what notes from the C scale "work" with this chord and which do not? Now play the G chord and look for notes which will work with that chord. What did you discover?

Improvisation

Improvisation is the practice of acting and reacting, of making and creating on the spur of the moment and in response to a stimulus of one's immediate environment. Or, we can say, it is playing something similar or contradictory to the melody following your imagination.

Modes and Scales

As you know by now, a **scale** is the name for a series of notes running up and down in a stepwise fashion. You have learned the scale of C major, but there are many other scales, too.

Scales in ancient times called modes can be traced back to Greek origins, where different cities evolved different modes (Ionian, Dorian, Phrygian, Lydian, Mixolydian, Aeolian and Locrian). The Greek scales ran down from a tonic note (rather than up, which is the modern method) and maintained certain intervals between notes. Two of the scales gave rise to the modern major (Ionian) and modern minor scales (Aeolian). Each scale started on a different note and _descended_ by characteristic intervals. In the middle ages, the church adopted these scales, made them _ascending_ from a tonic note and renamed them as modes.

We are going to work with them next year, but now let us look at the pentatonic scale. The pentatonic scale is probably the most frequently used scale, especially in pop and folk music. There are two main types of pentatonic scale, major and minor. Both consist of five tones. We can find also many ethnic pentatonic scales all around the globe. Here is one of them:

PENTATONIC E MINOR -

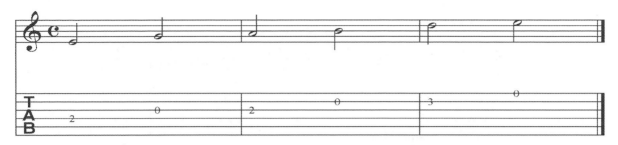

THIS IS ALL THE NOTES YOU CAN USE IN THE FIRST POSITION

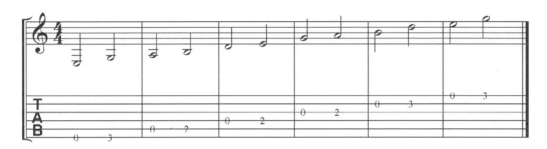

Practice this scale many times until you can play it with ease. Based on this scale, you going start to improvise. So let's start:

Everybody start playing (tutti) a melody together a couple of times; then one student starts to **improvise** (that is, play something similar or contradictory to the melody, using only the notes from the pentatonic scale). Then the improvising student lets the teacher play chords Em7 –Am-Em7- B7. When this is finished, everybody starts playing again, and the next person starts to improvise, and so on. Try your best and have fun.

Now lets all play this melody:

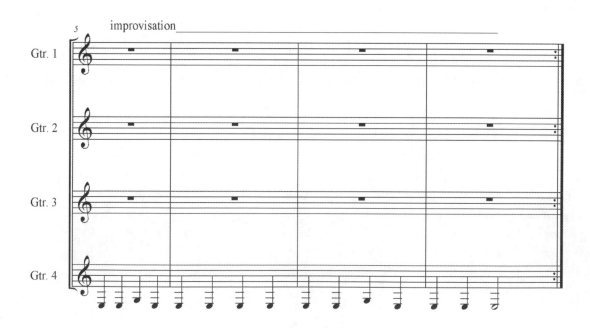

To make your improvisation even more interesting, try to play using different rhythms. Practice the following rhythmic exercises and then use what you have learned in your improvisation. Look also at exercises from Elements of Music 2 (student copy p.24).

Exercise 1

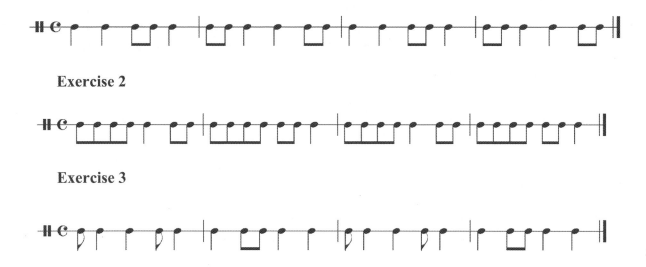

Exercise 2

Exercise 3

Composing Your First Song

Here is a chance to compose your first song. If you are working with a teacher, have the teacher play the chords while you play your own melody.

The first chord is, of course, C Major. Have your teacher or a friend play this chord for you while you improvise using sounds that are pleasing and interesting on the scale of C. Then ask your teacher to change to G chord and continue improvising, always using C Major Scale. Did you come up with a melody you like? If you did, then your song is based on two chords. You can experiment with your song. First play C chord (tonic) and listen for interesting notes for your first melody; than play G (dominant). You can also improvise in the opposite direction: first play your G chord, and then look for notes to follow, and finally resolve to C chord. You would be surprised how many songs in history are based on these two relationships Tonic-Dominant and Dominant Tonic.

If you are already familiar with the chords, take turns alternating between chords and notes. Use different rhythms for the chords and for the notes (strum the chords once for a couple of notes.) Now, it is inevitable that sooner or later you will play some wrong notes. Don't worry about it. If you can hear wrong notes, it is a good indication that you are developing an ear for what a pleasing melody sounds like.

Compose a piece

Now take your time to compose your first song using what you have learned in this lesson. Let your imagination guide you. Your first note is C, and you will progress towards G; next start from note G and finish on C. Begin and end with the correct notes. Be sure that you can play your melody on an instrument.

If you are not fully satisfied with the results, keep going. Every time, your song will sound better and better, and you will hear the difference. Have fun, be adventurous, and play with all your heart!

When you are satisfied with your first song, you can play it for the teacher and friends. However, do not stop, but rather keep composing new songs as you learn new chords, new scales, and new rhythms.

Compose a new piece based on the key of G Major. Use the same steps. Your first note is G, and you will progress towards D; next start from note D and finish on G. Be sure that you can play your melody on an instrument.

This is G Major Scale

```
G    A    B    C    D    E    F#   G
```

Basic chords for this key are:

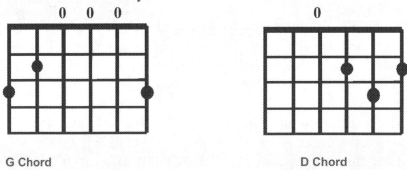

G Chord   D Chord

If you know more chords, you are welcome to use them in your composition assignment. When you have finished your first piece, share it with a partner. Ask your partner for feedback. What do you like about the composition? What do you think you can do to improve this composition? Switch partners, and get feed back from another person. How might you revise your composition based on the ideas you received from others?

Compose a new piece based on the key of D Major. Your composition should be eight measures in length. It should also Begin and end with the D note. Be sure that you can play your melody on an instrument.

This is D Major Scale:

D   E   F#   G   A   B   C#   D

Compose a new piece that uses dotted notes.

Compose a new piece that describes your favorite **animal** using whatever sounds and notes you want. Use dynamic marking.

Compose a new piece that describes the **weather** (rain, wind, storm, thunderstruck) using whatever sounds and notes you want. Use dynamic marking.

Compose a new piece that describes your favorite **story** using whatever sounds and notes you want. Use dynamic marking.

Compose a new piece that describes your favorite **picture** using whatever sounds and notes you want. Use dynamic marking.

There are some other chords to learn:

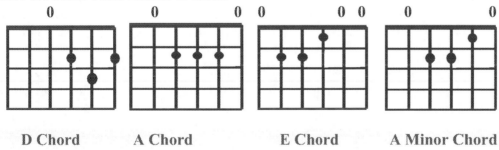

D Chord   **A Chord**   **E Chord**   **A Minor Chord**

Power chords
Guitar power chords are used extensively in all forms of rock music. Usually they consist of only two or three notes.

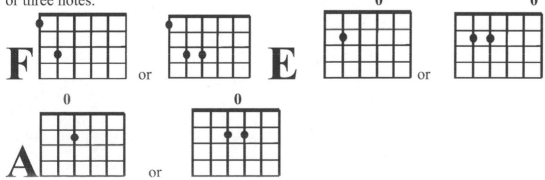

Unit 6: Elements of Music 3

Sharps and flats

♯	**sharp**	raises a natural letter name by 1 semitone (1 fret)
♮	**natural**	cancels the previous accidental, and returns the note to its natural unaltered value
♭	**flat**	lowers a natural letter name by 1 semitone (1 fret)

Key Signatures Using Sharps

Sharps or flats standing directly with a note are called accidentals. They affect only the notes which they immediately precede, and only those of the same letter in the same measure. However, sharps and flats can also be used with key signatures to affect all the notes with a given name.

For example, if there is one sharp immediately following the Treble Clef on the staff, F will always is played as **F#**. If there are five sharps in the signature, the respective notes will *always* be **F#**, **C#**, **G#**, **D#**, and so forth.

Here are the four key signatures that use sharps and the major and minor keys they identify:

1. G Major / E Minor
2. D Major / B Minor
3. A Major / F# Minor
4. E Major / C# Minor

Take the time to identify the sharps and use the process outlined above to work out the naming of the major keys yourself before proceeding to the next paragraph.

Performance Skills 3: Exercises Guitar I
EIGHTH NOTE ENCOUNTER

NEW NOTES TO LEARN C, B & D

For the C note, place your 1st finger at the first fret on the **second string** and press down. The B note is played on the open **second string**. You do not use any left hand fingers to play this note; you simply pick the third string. For the D note, place your 3rd finger at the third fret on the **second string** and press down.

SKIP TO MY LOU

Traditional

Hush Little Baby

Traditional

WILLIAM TELL

Giacchino Rossini (1792-1868)

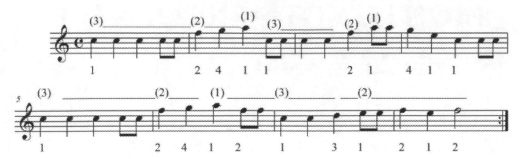

NEW NOTES

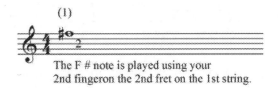

The F # note is played using your
2nd finger on the 2nd fret on the 1st string.

New Key Signature G Major

If there is one sharp in the signature, the respective notes will always be F#.

In the key of G Major

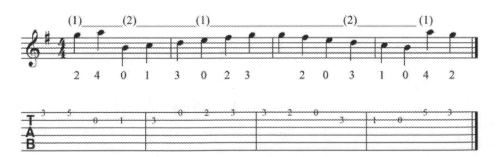

Tablature (TAB) is very popular among young people because it is very easy to understand. The six lines represent strings on the guitar the top one is the first string E, the second B, the third G, the fourth D, the fifth A, and the last one E. Numbers on the strings indicate which fret you are supposed to press.

GOOD KING WENCESLAS

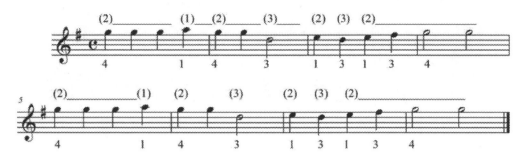

ALOUETTE

French-Canadian Folk Song

New Key Signature D Major

If there are two sharps in the signature, the respective notes will always be F#, C#.

In the key of D Major

ONE STEP AT A TIME

Traditional

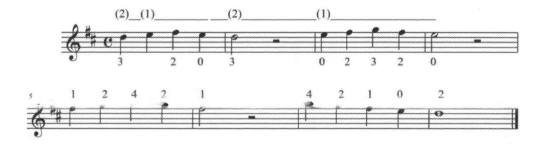

Performance Skills 3: Exercises Guitar II

EIGHTH NOTE ENCOUNTER

NEW NOTES TO LEARN A&G

A   G

For the A note, place your 2nd finger at the second fret on the **third string** and press down. The G note is played on the open **third string**. You do not use any left hand fingers to play this note; you simply pick the third string.

SKIP TO MY LOU

Traditional

Hush Little Baby

Traditional

WILLIAM TELL

Giacchino Rossini (1792-1868)

NEW NOTES

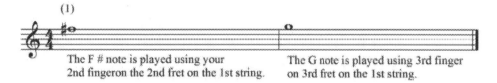

The F # note is played using your
2nd fingeron the 2nd fret on the 1st string.

The G note is played using 3rd finger
on 3rd fret on the 1st string.

New Key Signature G Major
If there is one sharp in the signature, the respective notes will always be F#.

In the key of G Major

Tablature (TAB) is very popular among young people because is very easy to understand. The six lines represent strings on the guitar the top one is the first string E, the second B, the third G, the fourth D, the fifth A, and the last one E. Numbers on the strings indicate which fret you are supposed to press.

GOOD KING WENCESLAS

Traditional

ALOUETTE

French-Canadian Folk Song

0   1 3   1 0 1 3 0   0

New Key Signature D Major

If there are two sharps in the signature, the respective notes will always be F#, C#.

In the key of D Major

(2)___   (1) (3)____   (2)_____   (3)____   (1)____   (2)

3   0   2   0   2   0   2   3   2   0   2   0   2   0 3

ONE STEP AT A TIME

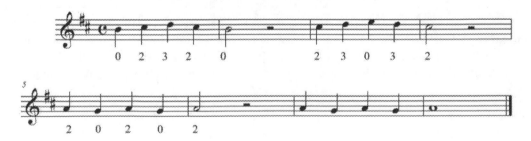

0   2   3   2   0   2   3   0   3   2

2   0   2   0   2

Performance Skills 3: Exercises Guitar III
EIGHTH NOTE ENCOUNTER

NEW NOTES TO LEARN F, E & D

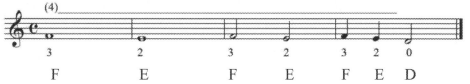

For the F note, place your 3rd finger at the four fret on the **four string** and press down. For the E note, place your 2nd finger at the 2nd fret (place your finger close to the 5th fret, but not on it, and press down. The D note is played on the open **second string**. You do not use any left hand fingers to play this note; you simply pick the third string.

SKIP TO MY LOU

Traditional

Hush Little Baby

Traditional

WILLIAM TELL

Giacchino Rossini (1792-1868)

NEW NOTE

The F# note is played using your 4th finger
on the 4th fret on the 4th string.

New Key Signature G Major
If there is one sharp in the signature, the respective notes will always be F#.

In the key of G
Major

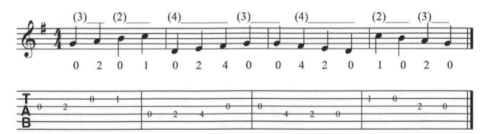

    Tablature (TAB) is very popular among young people because is very easy to understand. The six lines represent strings on the guitar the top one is the first string E, the second B, the third G, the fourth D, the fifth A, and the last one E. Numbers on the strings indicate which fret you are supposed to press.

GOOD KING WENCESLAS

Traditional

ALOUETTE

French-Canadian Folk Song

New Key Signature D Major
If there are two sharps in the signature, the respective notes will always be F#, C#.

In the key of D Major

ONE STEP AT A TIME

67

EIGHTH NOTE ENCOUNTER

NEW NOTE C

For the C note, place your 3rd finger at the third fret on the **fifth string** and press down.

SKIP TO MY LOU Traditional

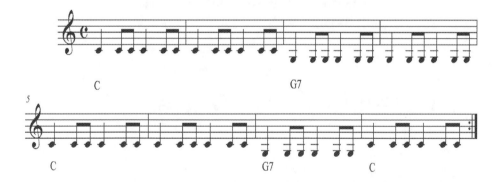

HUSH LITTLE BABY

Traditional

WILLIAM TELL

Giacchino Rossini (1792-1868)

NEW NOTES

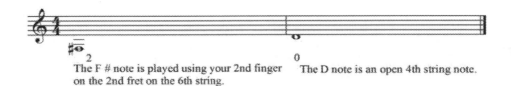

The F # note is played using your 2nd finger
on the 2nd fret on the 6th string.

The D note is an open 4th string note.

New Key Signature G Major

If there is one sharp in the signature, the respective notes will always be F#.

In the key of G Major

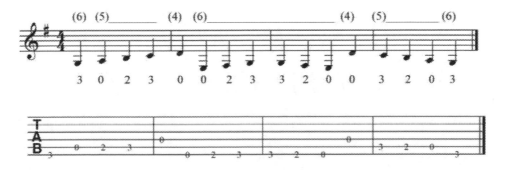

Tablature (TAB) is very popular among young people because is very easy to understand. The six lines represent strings on the guitar the top one is the first string E, the second B, the third G, the fourth D, the fifth A, and the last one E. Numbers on the strings indicate which fret you are supposed to press.

GOOD KING WENCESLAS

ALOUETTE

French-Canadian Folk Song

New Key Signature D Major

If there are two sharps in the signature, the respective notes will always be F#, C#.

In the key of D Major

ONE STEP AT A TIME

Traditional

Unit 7: Elements of Music 4

Dynamics

Standard notation uses Italian terms to indicate dynamics (the softness or loudness of a sound). The following terms come from Italian roots:

- *piano*: quietly; softly
- *forte*:   loudly; with force
- *mezzo*: half
- *issimo*: as much as possible

Here, in the order of increasing volume, are the six of the most common dynamics markings:

pp	*p*	*mp*	*mf*	*f*	*ff*
1	2	3	4	5	6

1.   *pianissimo:* play as softly as possible
2.   *piano:* play softly
3.   *mezzo piano:* play at a volume somewhere between soft and half-loud
4.   *mezzo forte:* play at a volume somewhere between half-soft and loud
5.   *forte:* play loudly
6.   *fortissimo:* play as loudly as possible

Please note that these markings are subject to varied interpretations, to say the least.

Anacrusis - Pickup Measures and Notes

Some songs start with incomplete measures. Notice that the first measure of the next song has only three beats (and notes.) These measures are called "pickup measures", and the notes are called "pickup notes." The missing beats from the pickup measure can usually be found in the last measure of the song.

When the Saints Go Marching In

(Student copy p.72)

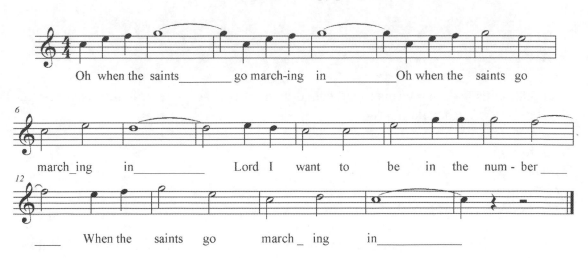

Tied Notes

Now let's take a look at tied notes. A tie is a curved line that connects two notes of the same pitch. The first note is played and held for the count of both notes (the second note is held but not played.) Ties are primarily used for notes that are held into another measure.

A whole note tied to a half note is held for 6 beats: 4 beats for the whole note plus 2 beats for the half note. A half note tied to a quarter note is held for 3 beats: 2 beats for the half note plus 1 beat for the quarter note.

Time Signature

Two numbers are placed at the beginning of a piece of music. The top number indicates the number of beats in each measure. The bottom number tells us which note gets the beat.

Performance Skills 4: Exercises Guitar I
CONCERT PIECES

WHEN THE SAINTS GO MARCHING IN
Exercise I

WHEN THE SAINTS GO MARCHING IN
Exercise II

WHEN THE SAINTS GO MARCHING IN
Traditional

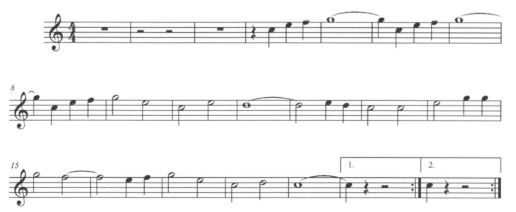

New Time Signature 3/4

The top number indicates the number of beats in each measure. The bottom number tells us which note gets the be

MINORE ROCK

To play this harmonics pick the string in your normal fashion. The left hand plays the harmonic by just touching the string directly above the 12th.

Pickup Measures and Notes

Some songs start with incomplete measures. Notice that the first measure of the next song has only three beats (and notes.) These measures are called "pickup measures", and the notes are called "pickup notes." The missing beats from the pickup measure can usually be found in the last measure of the song.

KUM BA YAH

"Kum ba yah" means "Come By Here" in the Gullah language, and is the title of a Christian hymn that originated in the lowlands of South Carolina. Gullah, a Creole blend of heavily-accented English and West African languages, was spoken by the African-American slaves living in the area. The melody is of African origin.

KUM BA YAH

Exercise I Rhythm

KUM BA YAH

African Folk Song

New Time Signature 2/4

The top number indicates the number of beats in each measure. The bottom number tells us which note gets the beat.

New Key Signature

If there are three sharps in the signature (A Major or F# Minor), the respective notes will always be F#, C#, G#.

AMIGOS
Exercise I new notes

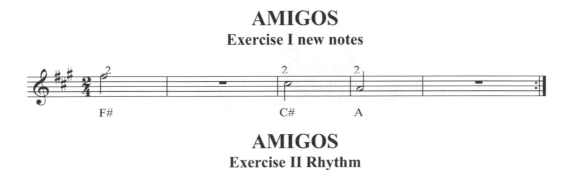

F#   C#   A

AMIGOS
Exercise II Rhythm

AMIGOS

Mexican Folk Song

Count Johann Anton Losy von Losinthal (c.1650-1720), famous Bohemian lutenist, inherited from his father in 1682 not only a vast fortune and estates, but also the high official rank of Councillor to the Bohemian Crown. Based in Prague, he traveled frequently to the Imperial capital, Vienna, where he combined his official duties with an active musical life, in which he encouraged interest in lute playing.

ARIA

Johan Anton Losy van Losinthal

NEW NOTES TO LEARN A&G

A   G

For the A note, place your 2nd finger at the second fret on the **third string** and press down. The G note is played on the open **third string**. You do not use any left hand fingers to play this note; you simply pick the third string.

SCARBOROUGH FAIR

Folk Song

Wolfgang Amadeus Mozart (January 27, 1756 – December 5, 1791) was a prolific and influential composer of the Classical era. His output of over 600 compositions includes works widely acknowledged as pinnacles of symphonic, concertante, chamber, piano, operatic, and choral music. Mozart is among the most enduringly popular of European composers and many of his works are part of the standard concert repertoire.

VARIATIONS ON A THEME BY MOZART

Wolfgang Amadeus Mozart

New Time Signature 6/8

The top number indicates the number of beats in each measure. The bottom number tells us which note gets the beat.

SPRING SONG

Wolfgang Amadeus Mozart

DANCE

Stanisław Mroński

Performance Skills 4: Exercises Guitar II
CONCERT PIECES

NEW NOTES

The E note is an open first string note. For the F note, place your 1st finger at the 1st fret The G note is played using your 3rd finger at the 3rd fret.

WHEN THE SAINTS GO MARCHING IN
Exercise I

WHEN THE SAINTS GO MARCHING IN
Exercise II

WHEN THE SAINTS GO MARCHING IN
Traditional

New Time Signature 3/4

The top number indicates the number of beats in each measure. The bottom number tells us which note gets the beat.

MINOR ROCK

Pickup Measures and Notes

Some songs start with incomplete measures. Notice that the first measure of the next song has only three beats (and notes.) These measures are called "pickup measures", and the notes are called "pickup notes." The missing beats from the pickup measure can usually be found in the last measure of the song.

KUM BA YAH

"Kum ba yah" means "Come By Here" in the Gullah language, and is the title of a Christian hymn that originated in the lowlands of South Carolina. Gullah, a Creole blend of heavily-accented English and West African languages, was spoken by the African-American slaves living in the area. The melody is of African origin

KUM BA YAH

Exercise I Rhythm

KUM BA YAH

African Folk Song

New Time Signature 2/4

The top number indicates the number of beats in each measure. The bottom number tells us which note gets the beat.

New Key Signature

If there are three sharps in the signature (A Major or F# Minor), the respective notes will always be F#, C#, G#.

AMIGOS
Exercise I new notes A, G#

For the A note, place your 2nd finger at the second fret on the **third string** and press down.
For the G# note, place your 1st finger at the first fret on the **third string** and press down.

AMIGOS
Exercise II Rhythm

AMIGOS

Mexican Folk Song

Count Johann Anton Losy von Losinthal (c.1650-1720), famous Bohemian lutenist, inherited from his father in 1682 not only a vast fortune and estates, but also the high official rank of Councillor to the Bohemian Crown. Based in Prague, he traveled frequently to the Imperial capital, Vienna, where he combined his official duties with an active musical life, in which he encouraged interest in lute playing.

83

ARIA

Johan Anton Losy van Losinthal

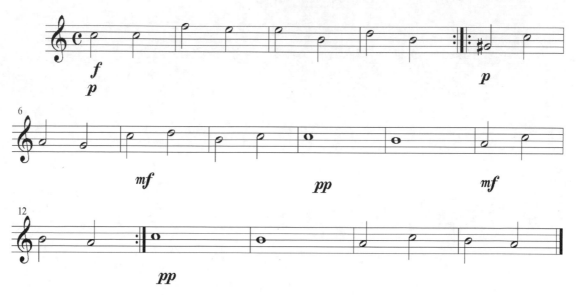

SCARBOROUGH FAIR

Folk Song

Wolfgang Amadeus Mozart (January 27, 1756 – December 5, 1791) was a prolific and influential composer of the Classical era. His output of over 600 compositions includes works widely acknowledged as pinnacles of symphonic, concertante, chamber, piano, operatic, and choral music. Mozart is among the most enduringly popular of European composers, and many of his works are part of the standard concert repertoire.

VARIATIONS ON A THEME BY MOZART

Wolfgang Amadeus Mozart

New Time Signature 6/8

The top number indicates the number of beats in each measure. The bottom number tells us which note gets the beat.

SPRING SONG Wolfgang Amadeus Mozart

DANCE

Stanisław Mroński

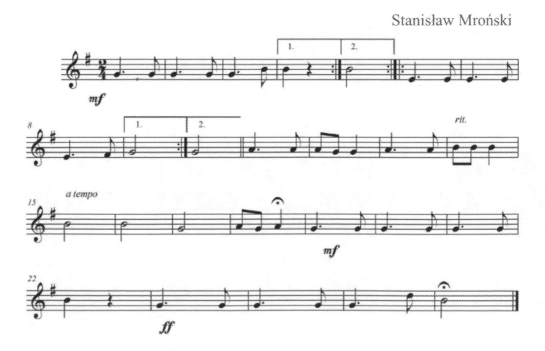

Performance Skills 4: Exercises Guitar III

CONCERT PIECES

WHEN THE SAINTS GO MARCHING IN
Exercise I

WHEN THE SAINTS GO MARCHING IN
Exercise II

WHEN THE SAINTS GO MARCHING IN

Traditional

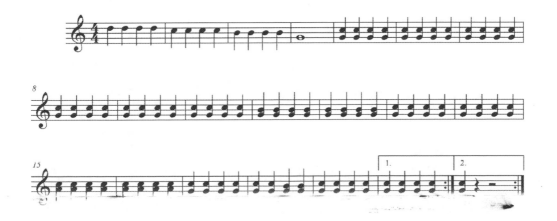

New Time Signature 3/4

The top number indicates the number of beats in each measure. The bottom number tells us which note gets the bea

Minor Rock

"Kum ba yah" means "Come By Here" in the Gullah language, and is the title of a Christian hymn that originated in the lowlands of South Carolina. Gullah, a Creole blend of heavily-accented English and West African languages, was spoken by the African-American slaves living in the area. The melody is of African origin.

KUM BA YAH

Exercise I Rhythm

KUM BA YAH African Folk Song

AMIGOS
Exercise I new note E

AMIGOS
Exercise II Rhythm

AMIGOS

Mexican Folk Song

Count Johann Anton Losy von Losinthal (c.1650-1720), famous Bohemian lutenist, inherited from his father in 1682 not only a vast fortune and estates, but also the high official rank of Councillor to the Bohemian Crown. Based in Prague, he traveled frequently to the Imperial capital, Vienna, where he combined his official duties with an active musical life, in which he encouraged interest in lute playing.

ARIA

Johan Anton Losy van Losinthal

SCARBOROUGH FAIR

90

Wolfgang Amadeus Mozart (January 27, 1756 – December 5, 1791) was a prolific and influential composer of the Classical era. His output of over 600 compositions includes works widely acknowledged as pinnacles of symphonic, concertante, chamber, piano, operatic, and choral music. Mozart is among the most enduringly popular of European composers, and many of his works are part of the standard concert repertoire.

VARIATIONS ON A THEME BY MOZART

Wolfgang Amadeus Mozart

New Time Signature New Time Signature 6/8

The top number "6" indicates the number of beats in each measure. The bottom number"8" tells us which note gets the beat.

SPRING SONG

Wolfgang Amadeus Mozart

DANCE

Stanisław Mroński

Performance Skills 4: Exercises Guitar IV

CONCERT PIECES

WHEN THE SAINTS GO MARCHING IN
Exercise I

WHEN THE SAINTS GO MARCHING IN
Exercise II

WHEN THE SAINTS GO MARCHING IN

Traditional

New Time Signature 3/4

The top number indicates the number of beats in each measure. The bottom number tells us which note gets the beat.

MINOR ROCK

KUM BA YAH

"Kum ba yah" means "Come By Here" in the Gullah language, and is the title of a Christian hymn that originated in the lowlands of South Carolina. Gullah, a Creole blend of heavily-accented English and West African languages, was spoken by the African-American slaves living in the area. The melody is of African origin.

KUM BA YAH

Exercise I Rhythm

KUM BA YAH

New Time Signature 2/4
The top number indicates the number of beats in each measure. The bottom number tells us which note gets the beat.

New Key Signature
If there are three sharps in the signature (A Major or F# Minor), the respective notes will always be F#, C#, G#.

AMIGOS
Exercise I: new notes:

AMIGOS
Exercise II Rhythm

AMIGOS

Mexican Folk Song

Count Johann Anton Losy von Losinthal (c.1650-1720), famous Bohemian lutenist, inherited from his father in 1682 not only a vast fortune and estates, but also the high official rank of Councilor to the Bohemian Crown. Based in Prague, he traveled frequently to the Imperial capital, Vienna, where he combined his official duties with an active musical life, in which he encouraged interest in lute playing.

ARIA

Johan Anton Losy van Losinthal

SCARBOROUGH FAIR

Folk Song

97

Wolfgang Amadeus Mozart (January 27, 1756 – December 5, 1791) was a prolific and influential composer of the Classical era. His output of over 600 compositions includes works widely acknowledged as pinnacles of symphonic, concertante, chamber, piano, operatic, and choral music. Mozart is among the most enduringly popular of European composers and many of his works are part of the standard concert repertoire.

VARIATIONS ON A THEME BY MOZART

Wolfgang Amadeus Mozart

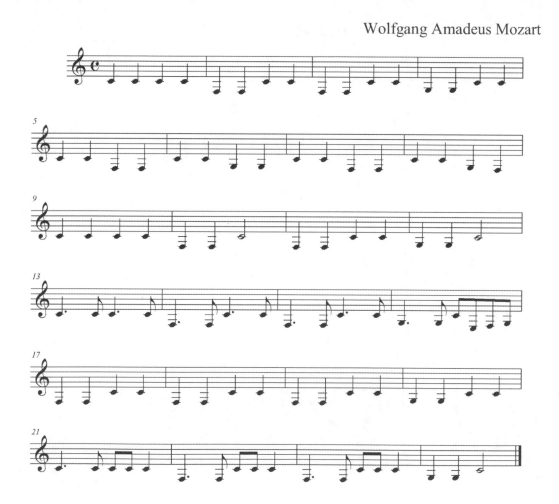

New Time Signature 6/8

The top number "6" indicates the number of beats in each measure. The bottom number "8" tells us which note gets the beat.

SPRING SONG

Wolfgang Amadeus Mozart

Dance

Stanisław Mroński

STUDENT HOME PRACTICE SHEETS

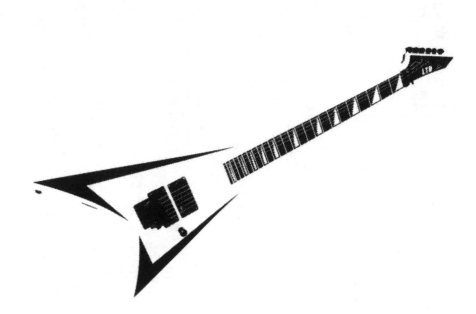

PRACTICE SHEET # 1

OBJECTIVES:
1. Learn the notes on the First String.
2. Practice counting.

The E note is an open first string note. You don't use any left hand fingers to play this note; you just pick the 1st string. For the F note, place your 1st finger at the 1st fret (place your finger close to the 1st fret, but not on it, and press down.) The G note is played using your 3rd finger at the 3rd fret.

Notes on the First String Exercise I

Notes on the First String Exercise II

Notes on the First String Exercise II

101

PRACTICE SHEET #2

OBJECTIVES:

1. Learn the notes on the second and first string.
2. Write in the counting beneath each line.

The B note is an open second string note. You don't use any left hand fingers to play this note, you just pick the 2nd string. For the C note, place your 1st finger at the 1st fret (place your finger close to the 1st fret, but not on it, and press down). The D note is played using your 3rd finger at the 3rd fret. Again, place your 3rd finger close to the fret but not on it.

POLKA

JINGLE BELLS

PRACTICE SHEET #3

OBJECTIVES:

1. Learn the notes on the third string.
2. Write in the counting beneath each line.

The G note is an open third string note. You don't use any left hand fingers to play this note; you just pick the 3rd string. For the A note, place your 2nd finger at the 2nd fret (place your finger close to the 2nd fret, but not on it, and press down). The B note is played on open second string.

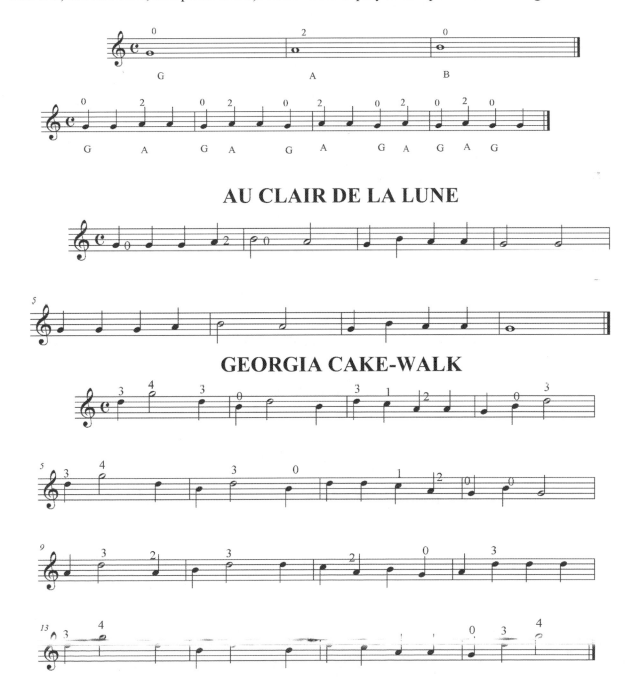

AU CLAIR DE LA LUNE

GEORGIA CAKE-WALK

PRACTICE SHEET #4

OBJECTIVES:

1. Learn the notes on the fourth string (D).
2. Write in the counting beneath each line.

Again the D note is an open fourth string note. You don't use any left hand fingers to play this note; you just pick the 4th string. For the E note, place your 2nd finger at the 2nd fret (place your finger close to the 2nd fret, but not on it, and press down). The F note is played using your 3rd finger at the 3rd fret. Again, place your 3rd finger close to the fret but not on.

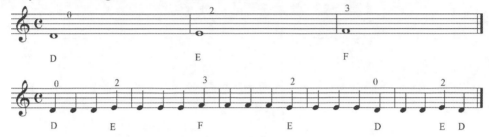

OLD MAC DONALD HAD A FARM

PIJE KUBA DO JAKUBA   Polish Folk Song

PRACTICE SHEET #5

OBJECTIVES:

1. Learn the notes on the fifth string (A).
2. Write in the counting beneath each line.

Again the A note is an open fifth string note. You don't use any left hand fingers to play this note; you just pick the 5th string. For the B note, place your 2nd finger at the 2nd fret (place your finger close to the 2nd fret, but not on it, and press down). The C note is played using your 3rd finger at the 3rd fret. Again, place your 3rd finger close to the fret but not on it.

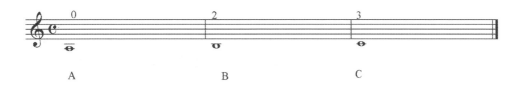

BUFFALO FROM THE PEG

VOLGA BOATMAN

PRACTICE SHEET #6

OBJECTIVES:

1. Learn the notes on the sixth string (E).
2. Write in the counting beneath each line.

The E note is an open sixth string note. You don't use any left hand fingers to play this note, you just pick the 1st string. For the F note, place your 1st finger at the 1st fret (place your finger close to the 1st fret, but not on it, and press down). The G note is played using your 3rd finger at the 3rd fret. Again, place your 3rd finger close to the fret but not on it. Try to use the tips of your fingers and make sure the notes ring cleanly after you pick them (no buzzing).

MORE NOTES TO LEARN

MARCH OF THE KING

Solo Pieces

This unit is designed to help you start your solo playing. Since your ability to play at this moment is greater then your reading skills, I provide you with an alternative notation called TAB (tablature).Tab is very popular among young people because is very easy to understand. The six lines represent strings on the guitar the top one is the first string E, the second B, the third G, the fourth D, the fifth A, and the last one E. Numbers on the strings indicate which fret you are supposed to press.

I recommend that all the students buy an introductory book for solo guitar to develop their individual guitar technique.

DANZA

107

WALTZ FOR ALEX

R.Tyborowski

COUNTRY DANCE

Fernando Carulli

SONG FOR THE NIGHT

111

SILENT NIGHT

Christmas Carol

GREENSLEEVES

Anonymous

SCARBOROUGH FAIR

Folk Song

SCALES

SCALE STUDIES - C MAJOR

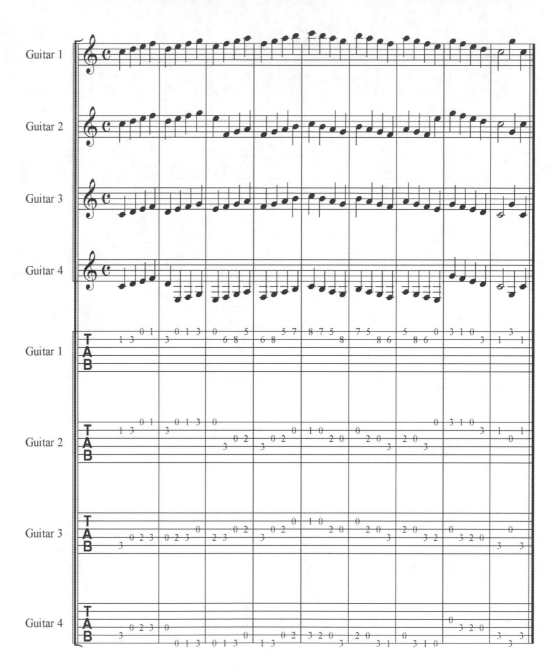

C MAJOR: C, D, E, F, G, A, B, C

SCALE STUDIES –G MAJOR

117

G- Major: G, A, B, C, D, E, F#, G

118

SCALE STUDIES – D MAJOR

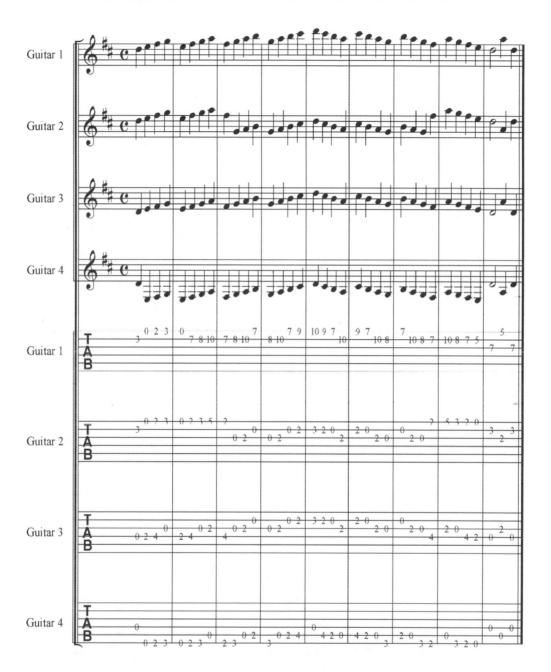

D MAJOR: D, E, F#, G, A, B, C#, D,

SCALE STUDIES - A Major

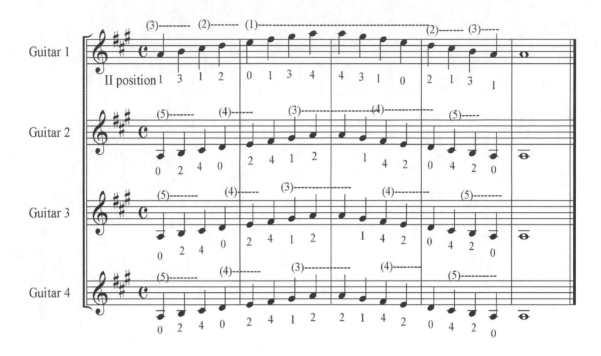

A MAJOR: A, B, C#, D, E, F#, G#, A

ALL NOTES ON GUITAR

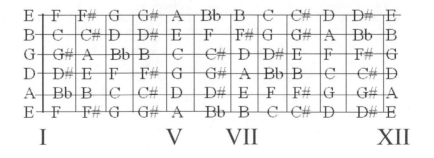

Student

Work

Sheets

WORK SHEET 1

NAME_____

1. Name parts of the guitar.

2. Give the letter name for each string.
   1st String _____
   2nd String_____
   3rd String _____
   4th String _____
   5th String _____
   6th String _____

3. Label the symbols below.

_____

𝄞 _____

4. How is the guitar tuned?

_____

_____

WORK SHEET 2

NAME_____

1. Label the symbols below.

_____

_____

_____

_____

2. Name the kind of guitars shown below:

_____

_____

_____

123

WORK SHEET 3

NAME_____

1. Name the chords below.

2. Label the symbols below.

♯ _____

♮ _____

♭ _____

𝄪 _____

♭♭ _____

3. Name the notes below.

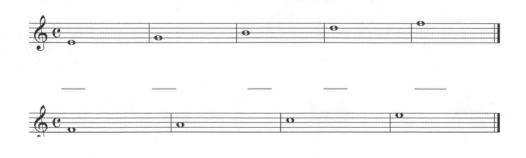

WORK SHEET 3 (student copy p.125)

NAME_____

1. Name the chords below.

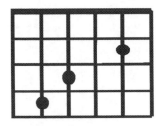   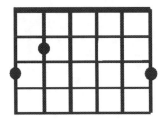

_____   _____

2. Label the symbols below.

♯ _____

♮ _____

♭ _____

𝄪 _____

♭♭ _____

3. Name the notes below.

WORK SHEET 5

NAME_____

1. Identify the Symbols.

pp _____
p _____
mp _____
mf _____
f _____
ff _____

2. Write the counting beneath the rhythm lines.

3. Below each note, write the correct finger and letter name.

FINGER _____   _____   _____

NOTE NAME _____   _____   _____

4. Fill in the blanks.

A musical sentence is called a _____
Draw a treble clef _____
Write two time signatures _____
Draw a sharp _____
The pinkie of your left hand is finger number _____

WORK SHEET 6   (student copy p.128)

NAME_____

1. Name the cords below.

_____   _____   _____

2. Write the counting beneath the rhythm lines.

3. Fill in the blanks.

Draw a whole note: _____, a half note_____, a quarter note_____.

The letter name of the 5th string is _____.

The middle finger of your left hand is number _____.

"Fine" means _____.

"Tempo" means _____.

4. On the back of this page, draw your left hand and label the fingers.

5. Draw the requested symbols.

Whole rest   Repeat sign

Half rest

Quarter note   Eight note

Whole note   Sharp

Treble clef

127

WORK SHEET 7

NAME_____

1. Below each note, write the correct finger and letter name.

FINGER   _____   _____   _____

NOTE NAME   _____   _____   _____

2. Label the symbols below.

3. Fill in the blanks.

"Fine" means _____.
"Moderato" means _____.
A curved line which connect two notes on the same space or line is called _____.
The letter name of the string 4 is _____.

How many quarter notes are in a measure of ³⁄₄ time? _____.

128

WORK SHEET 8   NAME_____

1. Write the counting beneath the rhythm.

_____

2. Write the counting beneath the rhythm.

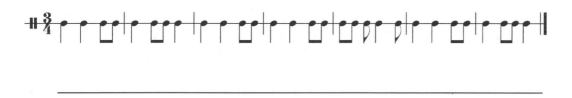

_____

3. Write the counting beneath the rhythm.

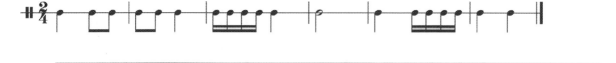

_____

MY
GUITAR
ENSEMBLE
PORTFOLIO

NAME_____

In this portfolio you will keep a record of your work in the guitar ensemble. The portfolio consists of four parts: recording of your performance, journal, home practice sheet, and demonstration of skills.

This is my work Tapes of a solo or group performances.

Date of Recording	Name of the recorded piece	Critiques
Date of Recording	Name of the recorded piece	Critiques
Date of Recording	Name of the recorded piece	Critiques
Date of Recording	Name of the recorded piece	Critiques
Date of Recording	Name of the recorded piece	Critiques
Date of Recording	Name of the recorded piece	Critiques

This is how I approached it.

My compositions. Record your compositions, either on tape or through invented graphic notation, simplified notation or standard notation.

_____
_____
_____
_____
_____
_____
_____
_____
_____
_____
_____
_____
_____
_____
_____
_____
_____
_____
_____
_____
_____
_____
_____
_____
_____
_____
_____
_____
_____

This is why I value it

Journal entries, pictures and comments

My first performance: Date and place of the first performance. What was the occasion? What did I like about the concert? Was I scared? What did my parents think about it? Could I do better next time? What would I like to change? Which pieces did I liked more than others and why? What did I learn from all that?

My evaluation

Teacher evaluation

_____

This is how I have changed.

_____

This is what I should work on next.

IV. Home practice sheet

Rubrics

There are two main areas of the guitar program that are assessed/evaluated with a rubric. Each level of the rubric explains what is required for that particular level.

	PLAYING ASSIGMENTS	PRACTICE RECORDS
NOT EVIDENT	Understanding of concepts and execution of skills is not evident.	Practice log is 70 minutes or less per week.
BEGINNING	Understanding of concepts and execution of skills is vague.	Practice log is 71-90 minutes per week.
DEVELOPING	Understanding of concepts and execution of skills is partially accurate.	Practice log is 91-120 minutes per week.
COMPETENT	Understanding of concepts and execution of skills is accurate but not fully developed.	Practice log is 121-149 minutes week.
SECURE	Understanding of concepts and execution of skills is accurate and fully developed.	Practice log is 150 minutes week.
EXCEPTIONAL	Understanding of concepts and execution of skills is exceptional.	Practice log is more than 150 minutes per week.

II. Demonstration of skills

When you practice think about these five factors.

In scale of 1 to 10 describe: what I think about my playing this week?

Notes accuracy				
Rhythm accuracy				
Quality of sound				
Dynamic				
Phrasing				

GUITAR MONTHLY PRACTICE SHEET

	SUN	MON	TUE	WED	THU	FRI	SAT	Total
WEEK 1								
WEEK 2								
WEEK 3								
WEEK 4								
WEEK 5								

Month: _____   Total : _____(in hours not minutes)

Student Signature: _____

Parent Signature: _____

GUITAR MONTHLY PRACTICE SHEET

	SUN	MON	TUE	WED	THU	FRI	SAT	Total
WEEK 1								
WEEK 2								
WEEK 3								
WEEK 4								
WEEK 5								

Month: _____   Total : _____ (in hours not minutes)

Student Signature: _____

Parent Signature: _____

GUITAR MONTHLY PRACTICE SHEET

	SUN	MON	TUE	WED	THU	FRI	SAT	Total
WEEK 1								
WEEK 2								
WEEK 3								
WEEK 4								
WEEK 5								

Month: _____   Total :_____(in hours not minutes)

Student Signature: _____

Parent Signature: _____

GUITAR MONTHLY PRACTICE SHEET

	SUN	MON	TUE	WED	THU	FRI	SAT	Total
WEEK 1								
WEEK 2								
WEEK 3								
WEEK 4								
WEEK 5								

Month: _____   Total :_____(in hours not minutes)

Student Signature: _____

Parent Signature: _____

GUITAR MONTHLY PRACTICE SHEET

	SUN	MON	TUE	WED	THU	FRI	SAT	Total
WEEK 1								
WEEK 2								
WEEK 3								
WEEK 4								
WEEK 5								

Month: _____   Total : _____(in hours not minutes)

Student Signature: _____

GUITAR MONTHLY PRACTICE SHEET

	SUN	MON	TUE	WED	THU	FRI	SAT	Total
WEEK 1								
WEEK 2								
WEEK 3								
WEEK 4								
WEEK 5								

Month: _____   Total :_____(in hours not minutes)

Student Signature: _____

GUITAR MONTHLY PRACTICE SHEET

	SUN	MON	TUE	WED	THU	FRI	SAT	Total
WEEK 1								
WEEK 2								
WEEK 3								
WEEK 4								
WEEK 5								

Month: _____   Total : _____(in hours not minutes)

Student Signature: _____

GUITAR MONTHLY PRACTICE SHEET

	SUN	MON	TUE	WED	THU	FRI	SAT	Total
WEEK 1								
WEEK 2								
WEEK 3								
WEEK 4								
WEEK 5								

Month: _____   Total :_____(in hours not minutes)

Student Signature: _____

GUITAR MONTHLY PRACTICE SHEET

	SUN	MON	TUE	WED	THU	FRI	SAT	Total
WEEK 1								
WEEK 2								
WEEK 3								
WEEK 4								
WEEK 5								

Month: _____   Total :_____(in hours not minutes)

Student Signature: _____

GUITAR MONTHLY PRACTICE SHEET

	SUN	MON	TUE	WED	THU	FRI	SAT	Total
WEEK 1								
WEEK 2								
WEEK 3								
WEEK 4								
WEEK 5								

Month: _____   Total :_____(in hours not minutes)

Student Signature: _____